Top Cat

Written by Sheryl Webster
Illustrated by Adam Gale

Cat is in a kit.

Top Cat!

Top Cat can
tap it up.

Top Cat can
nutmeg Kid.

Top Cat can nip
it in the net.

Can Kid run to get it?
Go, Kid, go! Kick it!

TOP CAT 9
Kick, Kid, kick!
No!
Kid can kick it.

Kid is top.
Cat is not.